IF YOU KNOW, YOU KNOW!

with Sonya

Wala'a Farahat
& Hoda Elshayeb

Illustrated by
Shireen Ahmed

If You Know, You Know with Sonya

Copyright @ 2022
Wala'a Farahat & Hoda Elshayeb

Illustrated by Shireen Ahmed

YGTMedia Co. Press Trade Paperback Edition

Published in Canada, for Global Distribution by YGTMedia Co.

www.ygtmedia.co/publishing

978-1-989716-59-5

All Rights Reserved. No part of this book can be scanned, distributed, or copied without permission. This book or any portion thereof may not be reproduced or used in any manner whatsoever without the express written permission of the publisher at publishing@ygtmedia.co —except for the use of brief quotations in a book review.

Printed in North America

Our Mission

To provide age-appropriate, representative, diverse resources for tweens and teens addressing themes of self-development, self-esteem, and identity.

Meet the Authors

Wala'a Farahat is a Registered Psychotherapist and cofounder of Rubiks Counselling Services. Rubiks Counselling Services is an organization shifting how mental health services are provided to diverse populations through accessible and culturally responsive education and therapy. She has extensive experience working with refugees, newcomers, and BIPOC communities, and she has worked in various community settings as a brief walk-in counselor, long-term therapist, trainer, and researcher. Her research interests include refugee mental health, trauma, migration, identity, racism, and spirituality. Wala'a provides services in English and Arabic to adults, youth, children, and families.

Hoda Elshayeb is an educator and life coach with more than 15 years of experience in teaching as well as mentoring in elementary schools and youth centers. She has a wealth of experience in organizing and leading school-wide activities, programs related to character education, and community outreach. Hoda has led and piloted projects focused on self-esteem, teamwork, leadership, and student empowerment. She has volunteered in orphanages and various community centers by tutoring children of different age groups. As a life coach, she offers one-on-one and group coaching with a focus on mindset, and she is passionate about running habit-change programs that foster deep-rooted achievement.

Contact Us

Feel free to get in touch to schedule a consultation, book reading, workshop, or custom package to meet your needs!

iykyk_teens   IYKYK Teens   iykyk.edu@gmail.com

www.iykykteens.com

Puberty

"In health class, we learned that puberty is when we all start becoming adults, but that made no sense! A couple of girls in my class had already gotten their period, and they definitely weren't adults!"

The truth is, when this happens, it doesn't mean you're an adult. Actually, you're not expected to act like one! Just continue being you and do the things you enjoy!

Puberty

Puberty: a stage in your life when your body is going through many changes, both on the inside and outside, to get you ready to be an adult one day.

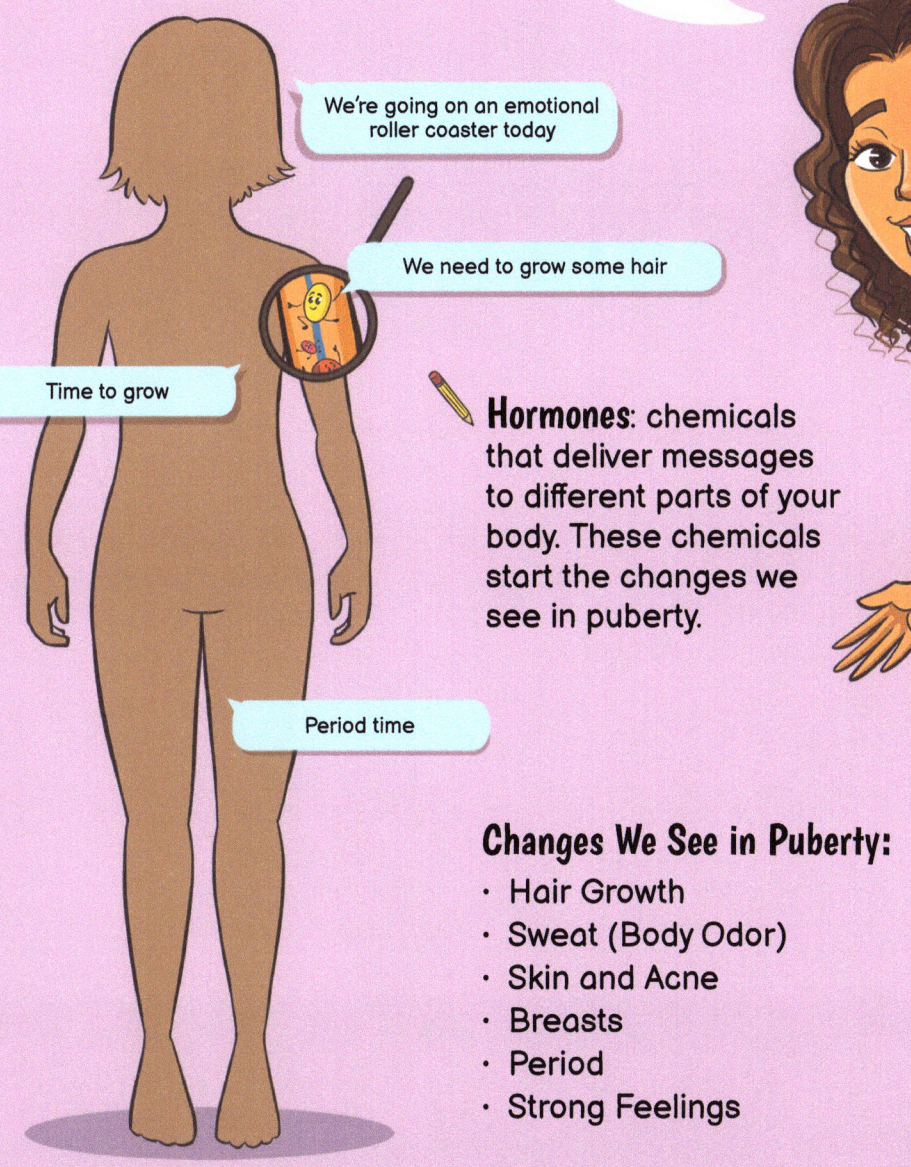

Hair Growth

One sign of puberty is that hair grows in different parts of your body. The hormones responsible for this are called androgens. The hair that grows in the underarm and private area is coarser than the hair on the rest of your body.

We were in fourth grade math class, and Mike, a boy who sits next to me, asked me why my arms look like his dad's arms! I mean, what was I supposed to say to that! I didn't let it get to me, but when I looked down at my arms, they sure had way more hair than Mike's arms did! My sister, who is a year older than me, didn't have as much hair on her arms either!

To be honest, it was swimming class that was the most awkward because I had some underarm hair that was starting to really show! I was starting to grow hair everywhere! Like even down there! Most of the girls in my class didn't really have any on their arms or legs except for a couple who also had a visible mustache! I remember how this one kid used to think it was funny to call them the "mustache girls," and I can only imagine how hurtful that must have been! I mean, Mike's comment made me feel uncomfortable too!

It's never okay to make others feel uncomfortable by making comments about their appearance. If you are in a situation where someone is making you feel uncomfortable with their comments or actions:

- Tell them that you don't find it funny and that they need to stop.
- If that doesn't work, talk to an adult about it. Sometimes you need to try more than once to find the right person. It could be a supportive teacher, school counselor, parent, or family member.

Did you know that the hair you grow actually protects your skin from external factors, such as the sun, and it regulates your body temperature? I told you it was fascinating!

Hair Removal Options

When your body is ready, you'll notice hair growth in your private area and in your armpits. Some people choose to remove this hair, and others don't. This is something you can talk to your parents about to decide if and when hair removal is the right option for you. If you do choose to remove it, there are different ways to do that.

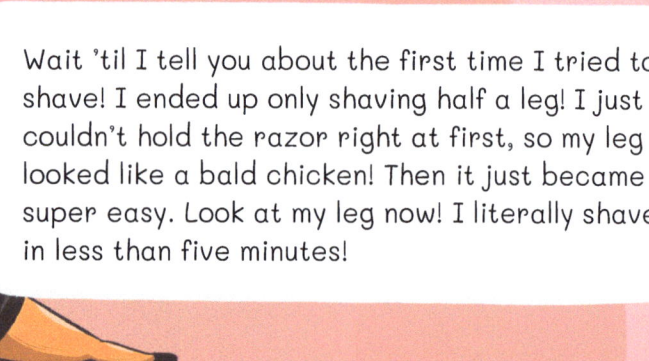

I personally make it a habit to regularly remove the hair, especially since I have a lot of it! I find that when I shave the hair in my armpits and private area, it really helps me stay fresh and avoid unpleasant smells.

Wait 'til I tell you about the first time I tried to shave! I ended up only shaving half a leg! I just couldn't hold the razor right at first, so my leg looked like a bald chicken! Then it just became super easy. Look at my leg now! I literally shave in less than five minutes!

Shaving

1. Get a parent or adult's help to purchase a razor.
2. Wet the area you're shaving really well. It's best to leave it under running water for some time so it's easier to shave.
3. Lather the area with soap or shaving cream.
4. Start by shaving in the same direction the hair grows, then shave in the opposite direction. Be careful not to cut yourself, but don't worry if you get a small cut—just wash it well and use a bandage, if needed.
5. Rinse off your leg and put some cream on it.

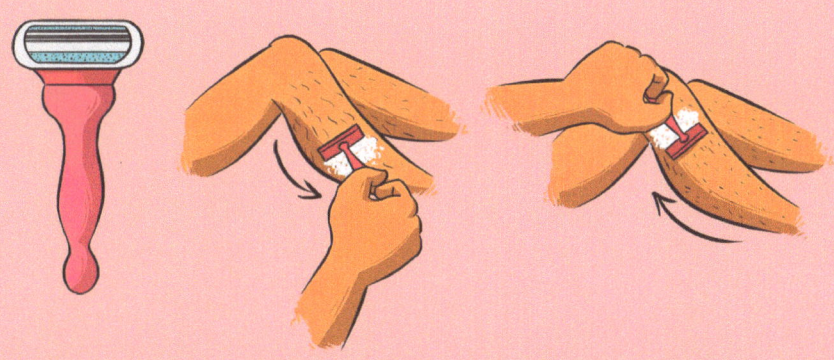

Note: Make sure you rinse your razor, cover it, and store it safely. Replace the blade regularly (every two to three weeks) because using a razor for too long can make your skin bumpy and red.

Waxing

1. Purchase wax or make it at home.
2. Spread the wax on the area where you'd like to remove the hair.
3. Use a piece of cloth or thick paper and spread it over the sticky wax (thin paper may rip and not do the job).
4. Quickly pull off the cloth or paper in the opposite direction of the hair growth.
5. Apply a soothing moisturizer (like aloe vera) to your skin.

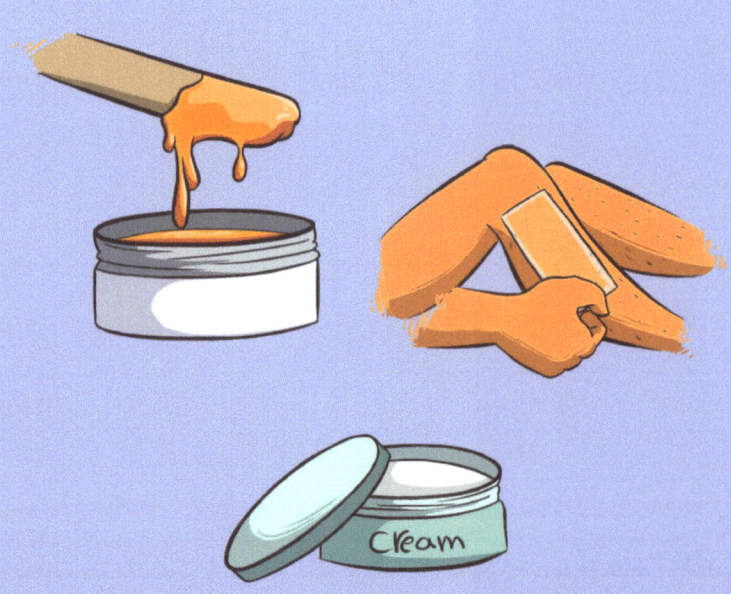

It's important to realize that each person has their preferences and own experiences throughout their puberty journey. There isn't one right way to do things, and it's important not to judge people for their choices.

Sweat (Body Odor)

Remember those little messenger hormones? One of the ways they manage our body temperature is through sweating!

> Isn't it cool how our bodies have their own cooling system? They cool themselves down by sweating! I know, I know, the smell is gross, but we can do something about that.

So, what causes our sweat to smell?
We have bacteria all over our skin. We also have apocrine sweat glands in our armpits, breasts, and private area that release fats and proteins. When the bacteria feeds on the fats and proteins, an unpleasant smell is produced by the bacteria's waste. In other words, the sweat itself is mostly water and has no smell at all!

Staying Fresh

It's important that we clean our bodies with water and soap so that we don't smell. There are some areas in our bodies that are more prone to cause an unpleasant odor when sweating. Those areas require cleaning and washing more regularly than the rest of the body. We don't just sweat from our armpits; we can also get sweaty down there.

 Body Odor Alert

- armpits   - private part   - feet

You know what smells gooooood, though? This pasta! Yuuuum.

Armpits

You may notice that there is still a smell, even after cleaning your armpits. This may be because there's sweat on your bra. Make sure to change your bra regularly. Dried up sweat stains can still create a smell.

Even when washing your armpits and regularly changing your bra, once you hit puberty, you will find that the sweat under your arms will have an unpleasant scent, and this is when deodorant comes in handy.

 antiperspirant (reduces the amount we sweat)

 deodorant (adds a pleasant smell)

Having sweat stains doesn't mean you're doing something wrong. I remember the sweat stains drove me crazy! I would clean under my arms, change my bra, and put on deodorant, and I'd still have these wet spots under my arms! I still get them sometimes. There's not much I can do except change when I can and throw my shirt in the laundry when I get home.

Feet

As you get older, and throughout your years of puberty, you may start to notice that your feet smell, especially when you play sports. Once you get home, wash your feet with soap and water, and don't wear the same pair of socks twice. If you find that your shoes are smelly, you should place them in a cool place to air out. Sometimes, putting some baking soda in them can help keep them fresh.

Private Area

To keep your private area fresh, it's important to wash and dry this area and make it a habit to change your underwear regularly.

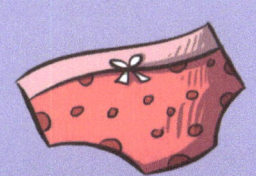

Skin & Acne

See this little guy right here? He usually shows up when I have my period. I only get a pimple or two now, right before that time of the month, but it wasn't always like this. When I was in grade 8, my face was full of these, they were itchy and red, and I was sooo embarrassed! It can really be frustrating! I tried facial wash and creams, and nothing seemed to work. So, I went to my doctor, and she sent me to see a dermatologist (a doctor that specializes in skin problems). It took some time before I started to notice my skin getting clearer, but it did eventually. I remember talking to someone about how the whole process was really getting to me, and that helped me feel better.

Acne: a skin condition that almost all people experience at different points in life, where red inflamed spots appear on the skin, known as pimples. Many will experience acne during puberty, while others get it as adults.

Pimples: small, hard, inflamed parts on skin that are symptoms of acne.

Where does acne come from?

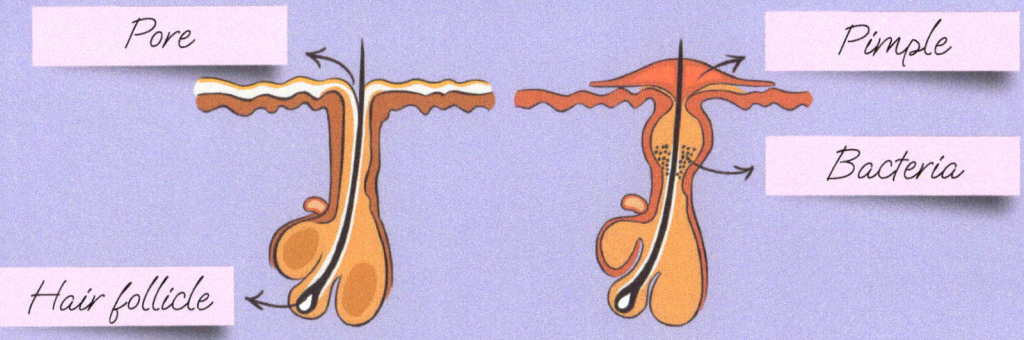

Our skin has small openings called pores that release oils and sweat. The skin also makes sebum, its own natural moisturizer, that keeps our skin soft. Sometimes sebum mixed with bacteria can clog the pores to make a pimple. It's important that we keep our skin clean and try not to touch our face often so we don't spread bacteria all over it.

It can be tough when you can't hide the pimples and your skin just doesn't look the same. Remember to cut yourself some slack and that most people get pimples at one point in their life or another. Those pimples won't last forever, and there is something we can do about it, like applying skin-care products or seeing a dermatologist. It also helps to express how you're feeling to a friend or adult that you trust.

Some Causes of Acne

Genetic

Environmental

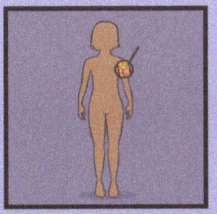
Hormonal

Nutrition

Skin Care

I just found it super hard to resist popping those pimples until I found out that it actually made the acne worse because the pimples would spread, and I'd end up with a little scar! I have this really cool skin-care ritual now, where I try to apply facial masks with my sister every other week! We call it our spa night! It's really relaxing and a lot of fun too! I honestly only started that a couple of years ago. I never really used facial masks when I was younger.

Tips for Skin Care:

- Wash your face gently with lukewarm water using mild soap or a cleanser once or twice a day. Avoid scrubbing; it can irritate your skin even more. Pat it dry.
- Avoid popping any pimples, because as tempting as it may seem, this can cause scars.
- Make it a habit to change your pillowcases regularly, and frequently wash any facial towels you use to avoid skin reactions due to bacteria.

What?! Why aren't you laughing? It's a good one!

What's more annoying than a stubborn pimple? Two stubborn pimples!

Breasts

You will notice your breast area start to grow during puberty. Breast development can happen before or after you see hair growth in your armpits and private area. Remember, there is no right order; each body is unique and will develop in its own unique way.

My breasts took a while to start growing compared to my friends in class. I had hair growing everywhere before my breasts started to appear. I honestly felt a little left out when the girls in class started talking about the bras they bought and how they were really excited when they went bra shopping! I heard that a lot of girls start to see breasts before hair growth, but that definitely wasn't the case for me. One of my friends in sixth grade had breasts that were significantly bigger than all the other girls. She told me how that made her feel very uncomfortable. I remember her saying that she felt embarrassed, especially if she had to run, and it made her not want to participate during gym class.

Looking back at those years of puberty, I can tell you now that although there were times that might have been confusing, the best part was having friends who would listen and be supportive. That really made all the difference, so remember to be that person who supports her friends and that a kind word goes a long way.

Breast Development:

- When breasts start to develop, this may cause the breast area to be tender, sore, and sometimes itchy. This is a good time to start wearing a training bra.

- It is completely normal for one breast to develop faster than the other.

- If your breasts are growing at a fast rate, you may notice stretch marks. Sometimes veins are also visible. It's nothing to worry about.

- Breasts develop in different sizes and shapes, and nipples also differ in color. Breasts can develop between the ages of eight and thirteen and can continue to develop until your early twenties.

Just like we have different features, heights, and sizes, our breasts are also different in the way they develop. Remember that this is not a race, and no one is ahead or behind. Each body grows in its unique and special way.

Bras and Sports Bras

Bras come in many colors and styles. Many girls are excited about buying bras, while others are more comfortable wearing sports bras.

✏️ **Check out** the "Sticky Situations" section at the end for what to do until you purchase a bra.

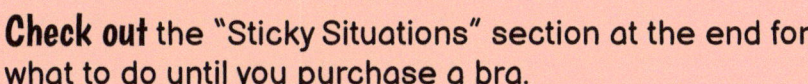

Bra shopping was interesting! My go-to was always the sports bras because I found them more comfortable, and I always got them in funky colors. My sister liked fancy bras with the underwire. Honestly, it really is a personal preference.

Period

So, everyone tells us that puberty and periods mean we're growing up, but how does getting my period every month help me grow up? It's actually pretty interesting. Your body starts training to prepare you for things way before, kind of like how we train to ride a bike. First, we start with training wheels, then two wheels, next on the sidewalk, and once we are older and have had enough practice, we are ready to bike on the side of the road. So, back to the period. Our period practices making our body baby-proof so that one day when we are older and have had enough practice, we may get pregnant if we choose to.

The uterus is between your hips and under the lower part of your stomach. On either side of the uterus there are ovaries that protect the eggs that you are born with.

Every month one of your ovaries will release an egg. This egg then travels down a tube (fallopian tube) and heads to the uterus. Meanwhile, the uterus prepares a lining that is thick and comfy and filled with nutrients to create a home for a baby in case pregnancy takes place (baby proofing). When there is no pregnancy, the uterus sheds this lining, and it then leaves through your vagina as your period. Even though you get your period years before you're at a stage to even consider having a baby, it's just your body's way of practicing and getting rid of tissue that is no longer needed.

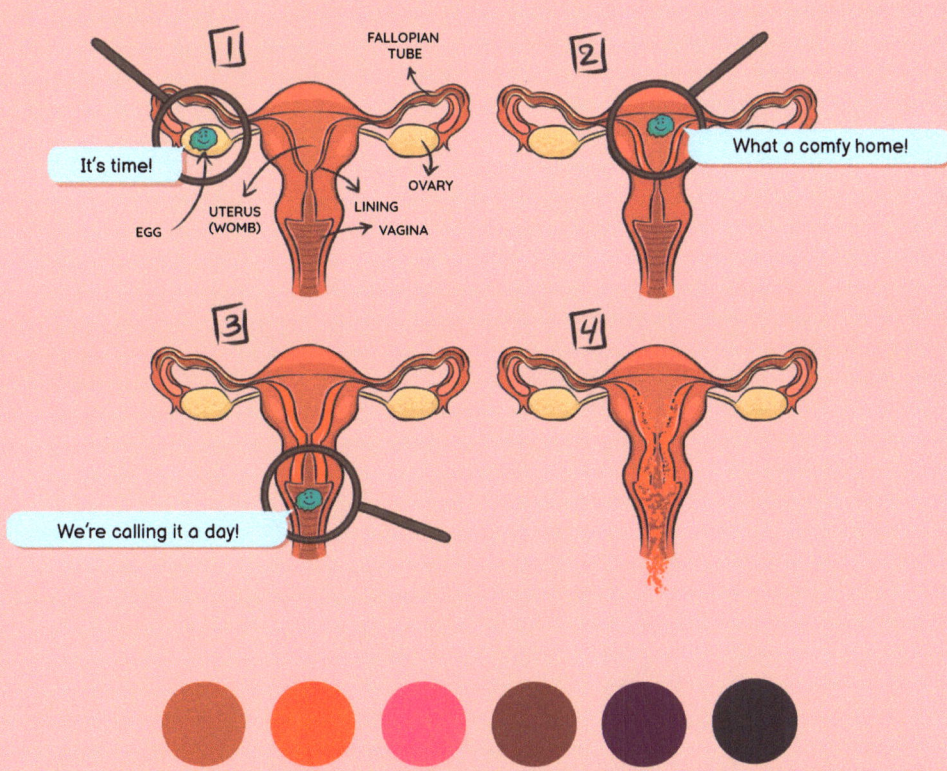

The blood that's discharged during your period can be different colors, and the amount of blood lost is two to four tablespoons, even though it can sometimes seem like a lot more.

First Time

You should hear the number of "first time" period stories I've heard! It can happen anywhere! In class, at home, on a camping trip, or while you're asleep. I got my period while I was at school. I went to the washroom during lunch recess and there was blood in my underwear. You know how shocking that was? I was so nervous and grossed out then, but now I know it's normal. I ended up rolling up some toilet paper and putting it in my underwear. After that, I asked a teacher for help, and she gave me a pad to use. Remember that there's nothing to be ashamed of, this is just your body doing what it needs to do to prepare you for the next stage in your life.

 **Check out** the "Sticky Situations" section at the end for ways to prepare for the first time!

Pads

Pads are made of a material that absorbs the blood that comes out. They have a sticky side that goes on your underwear to keep them in place. It's important to change the pad every couple of hours so the blood doesn't leak on your underwear or where you are sitting. Most people are more comfortable with trying pads first.

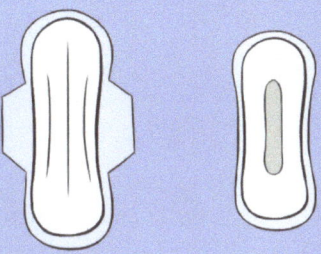

Tampons

Tampons are also made from material that absorbs the blood, but they're used on the inside instead of the outside. A tampon is put inside your vagina to absorb the blood and stop it from coming out. There is a string at the bottom that you pull to remove it. Like a pad, it's important to change your tampon every two or three hours. Leaving a tampon inside your body for too long can give you an infection and make you sick.

Menstrual Cups

Most menstrual cups are reusable, unlike pads and tampons. The menstrual cup is put into the vagina and does not absorb the blood but carries it in the cup. You should empty your menstrual cup two or three times a day. Like any product, menstrual cups have their pros and cons. They are eco friendly but can also be messy and may be difficult to use at first.

Sometimes you have to try more than one product before you decide what works best for you and what you are comfortable using. There are a variety of different options to choose from, so always read and learn about the product before using it. You can talk to an adult you trust to help you learn more about the different options.

What has wings but can't fly? A pad!

I used to regularly change my pads to avoid any leaking and to stay fresh, but there was this one time when I went on an apple-picking field trip with my class and did not have access to a washroom for a while. On top of that, I was wearing white pants! When I bent down to pick an apple off the ground, one of the girls in my class told me that she could see a bloodstain on my pants. I didn't know what to do and was so afraid everyone would notice. I went and told my friend, and I remember she was really nice about it. She gave me her hoodie to wrap around my waist. Later, I went to the washroom and found that it was a small spot, so I used wet wipes that I had in my bag to clean it. It was pretty hard to see the bloodstain after I wiped it, but I still kept my friend's hoodie around my waist for the day. After that day, I started keeping a pouch with underwear, wet wipes, and pads in my bag when I had my period. I still do that today. I call it my prep kit!

Check out the "Sticky Situations" section at the end for what to include in a prep kit.

Cleaning Up

- When you change your pad or tampon, wipe your private area (with wet wipes or some water on toilet paper), then dry yourself.

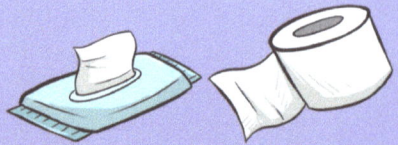

- Wrap your pad or tampon in the plastic wrapper it comes in or in a piece of toilet paper. Sometimes you'll find a garbage bin in the toilet stall, and sometimes it's outside of the stall. If the bin is outside the toilet stall, simply wrap your used pad and throw it out when you exit, but before washing your hands.

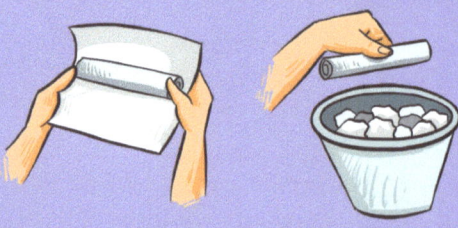

- Check the toilet seat for any blood spots and wipe the seat before flushing.

Sometimes I go to use the washroom and find a blood spot on the toilet seat. When my sister and I first got our periods, my mother showed us how to wrap our pads in toilet paper before throwing them away. It's okay if you've forgotten to wrap your pad before throwing it out, or if you left a little mess after yourself. Remember that anything that is new just takes a little bit of time to get the hang of.

Check out the "Sticky Situations" section at the end for how to deal with bloodstains.

Premenstrual Symptoms

✏️ **Menstruation:** another word for period; when the thickened lining of the uterus sheds in the form of blood from the vagina.

Some women get premenstrual symptoms. Premenstrual symptoms are symptoms women can have before and during their period. Many girls experience emotional or physical changes before their periods, and some do not. These symptoms could be due to hormonal changes.

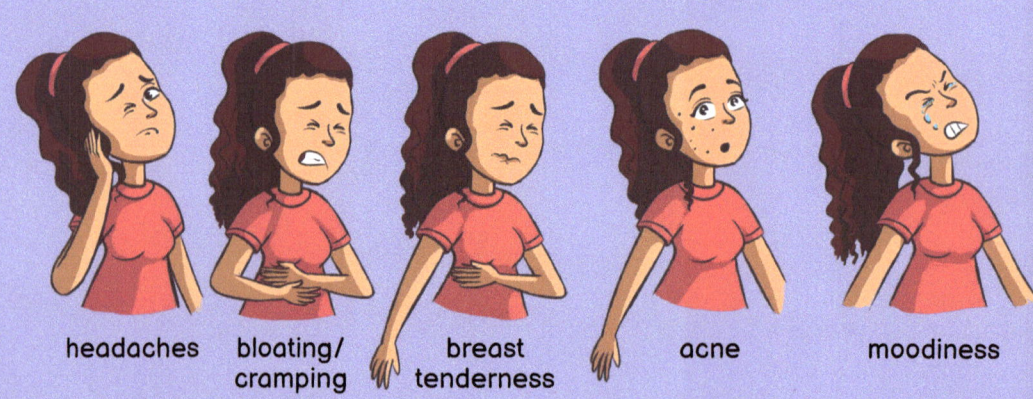

headaches   bloating/cramping   breast tenderness   acne   moodiness

Symptoms sometimes include different levels of stomach pain and can spread to the lower back and thighs. Some people also experience nausea, diarrhea, and dizziness. If the pain is very intense and gets in the way of your day, discuss what might help you feel better with your family doctor. You may need to try different things to see what works best for you.

Suggestions for easing menstrual pain

warm drink

heating pad

herbs

light movement

deep breathing

Last week I teared up and got emotional because I was running late for work and couldn't find my phone, only to find that it was in my back pocket all along! Then I realized that it was that time of the month! I, for one, always find that my mood is a little off right before I get my period. Things that usually wouldn't get to me or hurt me tend to get to me at that time. I also get cramps, so my stomach hurts for the first two days of my period. Drinking something warm like herbal tea or using a heating pad really helps me with the cramps! My sister doesn't get cramps at all but does get a headache.

What's a pad you never want in your underwear?
A heating pad!

Tracking Your Period

When I first got my period, it took me a while before I was able to know when to expect it. I used to wear pads days before I needed to because I was afraid I'd get it during class. Wearing pads for too many days can really irritate the skin in your private area! Then one of my friends told me that her mother used a calendar to track her period! I was in grade 10 when I started tracking mine, and I wish I had started earlier! It's so cool how tracking your period doesn't only help you know when to expect it, but it also teaches you so much about your body! I started off by using a calendar, but now I use this app. It's free, and it's got really cool features!

How to Track It

Tracking your period can be done using a calendar, a journal, or an app on your phone. A period usually lasts two to seven days. A cycle, which is from the first day of your period to the first day of your next period, is about twenty-eight days, sometimes more, sometimes less. It'll take a couple of months before you start to see a pattern and learn more about your body.

Some Points to Track

- First day: first day you see blood
- Last day: once the blood stops and you see no color
- PMS: symptoms related to your period. This can include cramps, headaches, mood changes, and diarrhea.

Calendars & Apps

When using a calendar, mark your first and last period day. You can draw an emoticon on your calendar to track how you're feeling on different days of the month. There are also many apps that are free that have several features allowing you to track your period. You will find that most apps give you the option to track the way you feel and other things you notice before, during, and after your period.

Journal

Using a journal is a great option because it gives you the space to write more. It can be like a mini diary where you express how and when you're feeling certain emotions. You write what days in the month you notice changes in the way you feel and describe those feelings. This way you're able to predict not only when you're getting your period but also the changes that come with it. If you're a little moody, you might realize that it's just that time of the month and it's the hormones doing their thing.

If you find that your period is irregular and difficult to track, don't worry. It could take a couple of years before your period starts to be regular. Some adults have irregular periods too, which can be due to several reasons. You should speak to your doctor about your irregular period because sometimes a change in diet or physical activity can help. And it's always a good idea to have a pad or tampon in your bag just to be prepared.

What does getting your period teach you?
To go with the flow.

Strong Feelings

People experience puberty differently. Some get more premenstrual symptoms than others, some might feel a little left out, others will experience feelings of discomfort. Some people may not experience any discomfort at all. We can feel confused and uninformed. We are all unique, and so are our experiences.

> Have you had a crush yet? I definitely remember my first crush! It made me feel all sorts of ways! It was hard because I didn't really want to talk to my mom about it, and my older sister never took it seriously! She always said I was just a kid, and it wasn't anything serious. But my feelings were real and serious!

We all have different feelings, and that's normal. Sometimes they're small and sometimes they're bigger. When feelings get really big or pile up, they can impact our thoughts and make it difficult for us to get things done.

During puberty, feelings tend to be strong because of all the hormonal changes our bodies are going through. We start to develop feelings that are new to us and sometimes it can become overwhelming having to deal with them all. We can start to have crushes, feel misunderstood, worry about whether we fit in, go through some bumpy friendships, and have strong feelings about things in general.

I remember when I was in grade 7, my grandma passed away. It was one of the most difficult moments of my life. I felt so sad, and the feeling didn't go away. Mom was also very sad and not doing well, and that worried me even more. Sometimes I'd have weeks when I didn't want to get out of bed, and it was really hard to get anything done. I had so many strong feelings and often felt alone with them and didn't know what to do. Trying to follow suggestions about skin care, tracking periods, shaving, and all this stuff was way too overwhelming. If you feel that way too, it's okay. It's important to not be so hard on yourself. You don't have to figure it out on your own. I know talking about how I felt and asking for help really made a difference for me.

Tip: If a friend shares strong feelings or something difficult with you and you're not sure how to help, remember that you can find an adult or professional to help. This could be a teacher, a parent, an older sibling, or a guidance counselor. You might want to brainstorm which would be most appropriate with your friend.

Just like physical health, we all have mental health, and it's just as important! Taking care of our mental health includes exercising, having good nutrition, practicing sleep routines, having healthy relationships, noticing our emotions, talking nicely to ourselves, and so much more!

Thoughts, feelings, uneasiness . . . sometimes it all gets overwhelming. When this happens, I stop and NOTICE.

Ugh! I can't stand it when that happens!
Nothing is going my way today!
I'm tired!

N - not alone
O - oak tree
T - temporary emotions
I - identify emotions
C - communicate emotions
E - extra practice

N- Not Alone 	I'm not the only one going through this; many others experience the same thing.
O- Oak Tree 	I'm like an oak tree with strong roots in the ground and a sturdy trunk. Stop, take a deep breath (breathe in from your nose and fill up your stomach like a balloon, then slowly breathe out from your mouth), and stand tall like an oak tree with your feet firmly planted on the ground. Imagine the roots holding you down.
T- Temporary Emotions 	I know the feeling will pass. It is only temporary. Feelings come and go; they don't last forever.

What comes and goes and sometimes feels like a roller coaster ride? Our feelings!

I- Identify Emotions 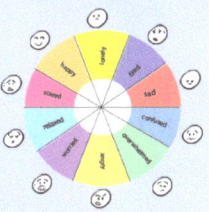	I name the feelings that are showing up for me right now. Sometimes there are more than one at the same time. For example, I could be feeling frustrated, angry, and confused all at the same time.
C- Communicate Emotions 	I communicate my feelings in different ways. I can do this by journaling or talking to a friend or someone I trust. Emotions can also be expressed through art (drawing, poetry, drama, dance, music), and in different communities of faith, they can be expressed through prayer or storytelling.
E- Extra Practice 	I am not discouraged if I don't feel better right away. It takes extra practice to learn to be there for myself.

If you find that applying all the "NOTICE" steps is too much, it's okay. You don't have to do them all. Choose the ones that work best for you depending on how you're feeling at the time.

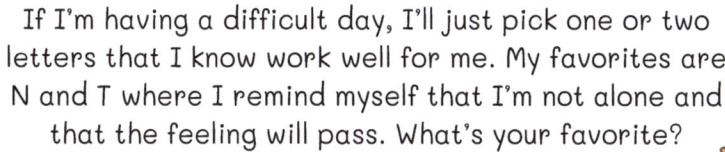

If I'm having a difficult day, I'll just pick one or two letters that I know work well for me. My favorites are N and T where I remind myself that I'm not alone and that the feeling will pass. What's your favorite?

Movement

When we move, "feel good" hormones are released, and this can boost our mood and increase our energy level. It can take some time and consistent movement before we feel the impact.

Some people love to play team sports and others prefer biking, skating, or going for a run. Make sure you're staying active by choosing what works for you and what you enjoy!

We all have different ways of moving, learning, and experiencing the world. Each of our bodies moves differently, and it's important to explore different variations of movements, sports, or exercises that work best for us. For example, engaging in chair exercises, power chair sports, or going on a walk using an aid.

I remember in grade 5 how I always looked forward to playing soccer during recess, but then some of the kids would get really competitive and our soccer games would turn into soccer fights. A couple of my friends and I chose to not participate anymore, but I really missed it! I talked to my gym teacher about the soccer fights, and he put down some ground rules and would sometimes coach the games during recess. I'm not going to lie, there was still some fighting, but it wasn't nearly as bad! Later that year, I joined the basketball tournament. I can't even remember who won, but what I do remember is that I really enjoyed the games! My sister didn't really like sports, but she loved skateboarding and would go almost every day after school!

What's a kind of exercise that isn't really helpful?
Running away from your problems!

Sleep Routine

Having a sleep routine really makes a difference in my day. For me, if I sleep for hours, but I don't get quality sleep, I still feel exhausted and really find it hard to wake up in the morning. When I study, watch an action movie, or stare at my phone right before bedtime, once I fall asleep, it's like my body is sleeping but my mind is still working! I used to drive my mom crazy because I couldn't get up on time in the mornings, and I'd always say, "Give me five more minutes" like ten times! Recently, I have made it a habit to do something relaxing before bedtime, and I try my very best to not look at my phone or laptop at least half an hour before I go to sleep. I'll write in my journal, do some yoga, or chitchat with my family, and it actually makes my sleep so much better! If you find you don't really have much energy in the mornings or feel a little moody, believe me, I know the feeling! So, why don't you try to experiment with a quality sleep routine by doing something relaxing that is electronic-free before bedtime and see how it works for you?

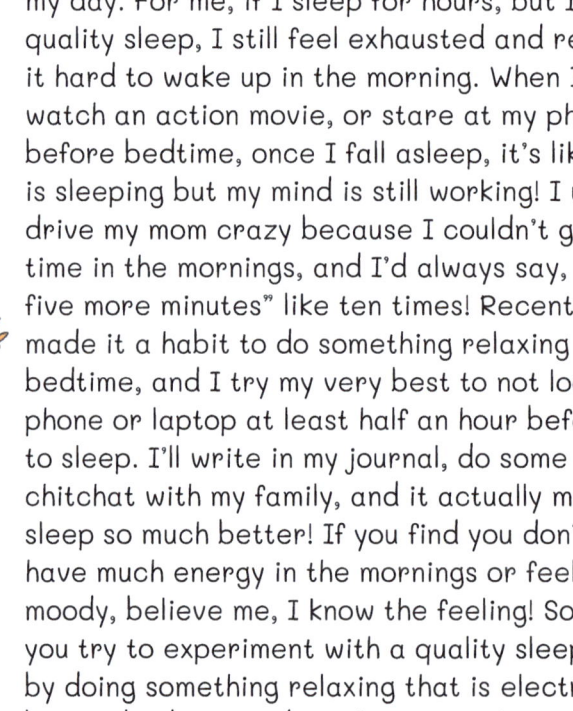

Getting enough sleep is very important because it impacts our growth and our overall mood. While we're asleep, our brain is hard at work! Growth hormones are traveling in our bodies, information is being stored and processed, and harmful substances are released. Sleep also keeps many other hormones balanced. When our hormone levels are irregular, it can impact our moods and how our body feels throughout the day.

Bedtime Routine

Privacy

My sister and I shared a room growing up and she would get mad at me if I didn't knock before entering our room. She'd always yell, "What if I was changing?!" Our mom would talk to us about how we should always respect each other's privacy. I even knew the meaning of the word consent when I was still in kindergarten because my mom would always use that word when she explained that while playing, we should not hold or touch someone without their consent. She also explained to us that our bodies are private and when something feels uncomfortable or not right, it's important to know that we can say no. Sometimes it's hard to do it and we may need to seek the help of an adult that we trust.

Consent: when you give your consent, you allow something or agree for it to take place.

Privacy does not start at the age of puberty, it starts from when you are a baby, but it looks different as you grow older and become more independent. Your body belongs to you, and it's never okay for anyone to ask about, see, or touch your private parts. Sometimes there's an exception; for example, if we need to show a doctor or talk to a parent about a health concern we have in that area.

Internal Clock

You will see that even though you and your classmates are all the same age, the changes you see in your body are not all happening at the same rate. This can sometimes make you feel left out, especially if other girls talk about the changes that you don't see yet. You may also feel like you are the first to experience those changes, which may be a little uncomfortable. Know that our bodies each have an internal clock and that you will see your body developing when it is ready. Talk to an adult or a friend about how you're feeling, but remember to speak to someone you trust, and make sure your sources of information are reliable.

The number of things I'd hear at school from other kids that totally made no sense are just countless! Some of the things that were said were true, but a lot of the girls were misinformed, including myself. I've always remembered the school librarian's words about making sure that your sources are reliable, and not only when doing research but also when speaking to those around you. Don't believe everything you hear and ask those who have more experience when in doubt. One of my friends was convinced that it wasn't safe for us to participate in sports during our period! I remember seeing my sister go skateboarding all the time when she had her period. So, I asked my teacher during health class, and she said that there was nothing wrong with being active at that time of the month, and that it's actually recommended to do so and can even sometimes relieve pain! The important thing I learned is to listen to my body, make sure to rest when I need to, and to stay hydrated.

Boys' Puberty

You know how I mentioned earlier that hitting puberty was confusing and there were so many changes? Guess what? Boys feel that way too! They go through different changes than we do because their bodies are different. You know how I said everyone is different and the changes happen at different times? Sometimes boys are taller or shorter, have more acne, less beard hair or more beard hair, all because they, too, are at different stages of hitting puberty.

Sticky Situations

1. Bloodstains

I stand up during class to borrow an eraser and my friend whispers, "There is a bloodstain on your pants!" How do I cover the blood stain?

    a. I wrap my hoodie around my waist or borrow one from a friend.

    b. I use wipes or a wet paper towel to try to remove the stain.

    c. I tell my friend she shouldn't have told me.

2. First Period and You're at School

I go to use the washroom during French class and notice a red spot in my underwear. I don't have a pad, and there is still a while before the school day ends. What should I do?

    a. Just ignore it and deal with it when I get home.

    b. Roll up some toilet paper and put it in my underwear until I can get a pad.

    c. Ask one of my teachers, a school counselor, or any adult at school for a pad.

3. Notice Nipples Showing Through Shirt and Don't Have a Bra Yet

I get to school and notice that my nipples are showing through my shirt! I don't feel comfortable. I think I'm going to talk to my mom about buying bras, but what do I do until I have a bra?

   a. Call my mom and tell her that we have to go bra shopping right now.
   b. Borrow my friend's baggy sweater to wear for the day.
   c. If I have a tank top or tight shirt, I wear it underneath so it isn't as obvious.

4. Have Cramps and Can't Participate in Gym Class

Gym class is about to start, and my cramps have been painful since the morning. Today, we are doing laps, and I really don't think I have it in me. What do I do?

   a. Participate in gym anyway because I have no choice.
   b. Take the teacher aside and let them know I'm not feeling well and need to sit this one out.
   c. Pick a fight so the teacher kicks me out.

5. Making your prep kit

I have been tracking my period and know it's coming in a couple of days, so I thought I'd prepare my prep kit. What should I include?

   a. Pads/tampons, wet wipes, extra underwear, deodorant
   b. Chocolate, an extra pair of socks, mascara
   c. Sticky note with "NOTICE" steps, pads/tampons, tissues

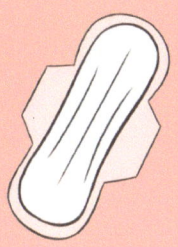

N - not alone
O - oak tree
T - temporary emotions
I - identify emotions
C - communicate emotions
E - extra practice

Glossary

- **ACNE:** a skin condition that usually occurs during the time of puberty that results in pimples

- **ADOLESCENT:** the time frame in life that starts from puberty until adulthood

- **APOCRINE SWEAT GLANDS:** glands that become active at the time of puberty and are found in certain parts of the body such as the armpits, breasts, and pubic areas

- **CONSENT:** when you give your consent, you allow something or agree for it to take place

- **DERMATOLOGIST:** a doctor that specializes in skin problems

- **HORMONES:** chemicals that deliver messages to different parts of the body; these chemicals start the changes we see in puberty

- **MENSTRUATION:** another word for period; when the thickened lining of the uterus sheds in the form of blood from the vagina

- **OVARIES:** two small oval organs that store eggs and are found in the pelvis

- **OVULATION**: when one of the ovaries releases an egg, this egg will travel down a tube (fallopian tube) and enter the uterus

- **PIMPLES**: small, hard, inflamed parts on skin that are symptoms of acne

- **PMS**: Premenstrual symptoms are symptoms that start before menstruation and can include stomach cramps, moodiness, and headaches

- **PUBERTY**: a stage in life when the body is going through many changes, both on the inside and outside, to get ready to be an adult one day

- **UTERUS**: the uterus is a muscular organ between the hips and under the lower part of the stomach. It develops a lining to create a home for a baby during pregnancy; if there is no pregnancy, the lining is shed through the vagina in the form of blood (period)

- **VAGINA**: a muscular tube that leads from the uterus to outside the body

STICKY SITUATIONS
ANSWER KEY

1. a and b;
2. b and c;
3. b and c;
4. b; 5. a and c

www.iykykteens.com